WHETHER OR NOT you are Catholic, you may have questions about the Catholic faith. You may have heard challenges to the Catholic Church's claim to be the interpreter and safeguard of the teachings of Jesus Christ.

Such challenges come from door-to-door missionaries who ask, "Are you saved? from peer pressure that urges you to ignore the Church's teachings, from a secular culture that whispers "There is no God."

You can't deal with these challenges unless you understand the basics of the Catholic faith. This booklet introduces them to you.

In Catholicism you will find answers to life's most troubling questions: Why am I here? Who made me? What must I believe? How must I act? All these can be answered to your satisfaction, if only you will open yourself to God's grace, turn to the Church he established, and follow his plan for you (John 7:17).

AN UNBROKEN HISTORY

Jesus said his Church would be "the light of the world." He then noted that "a city set on a hill cannot be hid" (Matt. 5:14). This means his Church is a *visible* organization. It must have characteristics that clearly identify it and that distinguish it from other churches. Jesus promised, "I will build my Church and the gates of hell will not prevail against it" (Matt. 16:18). This means that his Church will never be destroyed and will never fall away from him. His Church will survive until his return.

The Catholic Church is the only universal Christian Church that has existed since the time of Jesus. Every other Christian group is an offshoot of the Catholic Church. The Eastern Orthodox churches broke away from unity with the pope in 1054. The Protestant communities were established during the Reformation, which began in 1517. (Most of today's Protestant groups are actually offshoots of the original Protestant offshoots.)

Only the Catholic Church existed in the tenth century, in the fifth century, and in the first century, faithfully teaching the doctrines given by Christ to the apostles, omitting nothing. The line of popes can be traced back, in unbroken succession, to Peter himself. This is unequaled by any institution in history.

Even the oldest government is new compared to the papacy, and the churches that send out door-to-door missionaries are young compared to the Catholic Church. Many of these churches began as recently as the nineteenth or twentieth centuries. Some even began during your own lifetime. None of them can claim to be the Church Jesus established.

The Catholic Church has existed for nearly 2,000 years, despite constant opposition from the world. This is testimony to the Church's divine origin. It must be more than a merely human organization, especially considering that its human members—even some of its leaders—have been unwise, corrupt, or prone to heresy.

Any merely human organization with such members would have collapsed early on. The Catholic Church is today the most vigorous church in the world (and the largest, with a billion members: one sixth of the human race), and that is testimony not to the cleverness of the Church's leaders, but to the protection of the Holy Spirit.

FOUR MARKS OF THE TRUE CHURCH

If we wish to locate the Church founded by Jesus, we need to locate the one that has the four chief marks or qualities of his Church. The Church we seek must be one, holy, catholic, and apostolic.

The Church Is One
(Rom. 12:5, 1 Cor. 10:17, 12:13, CCC* 813–822)

Jesus established only *one* Church, not a collection of differing churches (Lutheran, Baptist, Anglican,

*CCC = Catechism of the Catholic Church

and so on). The Bible says the Church is the bride of Christ (Eph. 5:23–32). Jesus can have but *one* spouse, and his spouse is the Catholic Church.

His Church also teaches just one set of doctrines, which must be the same as those taught by the apostles (Jude 3). This is the unity of belief to which Scripture calls us (Phil. 1:27, 2:2).

Although some Catholics dissent from officially taught doctrines, the Church's official teachers—the pope and the bishops united with him—have never changed any doctrine. Over the centuries, as doctrines are examined more fully, the Church comes to understand them more deeply (John 16:12–13), but it never understands them to mean the opposite of what they once meant.

The Church Is Holy
(Eph. 5:25–27, Rev. 19:7–8, CCC 823–829)

By his grace Jesus makes the Church holy, just as he is holy. This doesn't mean that each member is always holy. Jesus said there would be both good and bad members in the Church (John 6:70), and not all the members would go to heaven (Matt. 7:21–23).

But the Church itself is holy because it is the source of holiness and is the guardian of the special means of grace Jesus established, the sacraments (cf. Eph. 5:26).

The Church Is Catholic
(Matt. 28:19–20, Rev. 5:9–10, CCC 830–856)

Jesus' Church is called catholic ("universal" in Greek) because it is his gift to all people. He told his apostles to go throughout the world and make disciples of "all nations" (Matt. 28:19–20).

For 2,000 years the Catholic Church has carried out this mission, preaching the good news that Christ died for all men and that he wants all of us to be members of his universal family (Gal. 3:28).

Nowadays the Catholic Church is found in every country of the world and is still sending out missionaries to "make disciples of all nations" (Matt. 28:19).

The Church Jesus established was known by its most common title, "the Catholic Church," at least as early as the year 107, when Ignatius of Antioch used that title to describe the one Church Jesus founded. The title apparently was old in Ignatius's time, which means it probably went all the way back to the time of the apostles.

The Church Is Apostolic
(Eph. 2:19–20, CCC 857–865)

The Church Jesus founded is apostolic because he appointed the apostles to be the first leaders of the Church, and their successors were to be its future leaders. The apostles were the first bishops, and, since the first century, there has been an unbroken line of Catholic bishops faithfully handing on what the apostles taught the first Christians in Scripture and oral Tradition (2 Tim. 2:2).

These beliefs include the bodily Resurrection of Jesus, the Real Presence of Jesus in the Eucharist, the sacrificial nature of the Mass, the forgiveness of sins through a priest, baptismal regeneration, the existence of purgatory, Mary's special role, and much more —even the doctrine of apostolic succession itself.

Early Christian writings prove the first Christians were thoroughly Catholic in belief and practice and looked to the successors of the apostles as their leaders. What these first Christians believed is still believed by the Catholic Church. No other Church can make that claim.

Pillar of Fire, Pillar of Truth

Man's ingenuity cannot account for this. The Church has remained one, holy, catholic, and apostolic—not through man's effort, but because God preserves the Church he established (Matt. 16:18, 28:20).

He guided the Israelites on their escape from Egypt by giving them a pillar of fire to light their way across the dark wilderness (Exod. 13:21). Today he guides us through his Catholic Church.

The Bible, sacred Tradition, and the writings of the earliest Christians testify that the Church teaches with Jesus' authority. In this age of countless competing religions, each clamoring for attention, one voice rises above the din: the Catholic Church, which the Bible calls "the pillar and foundation of truth" (1 Tim. 3:15).

Jesus assured the apostles and their successors, the popes and the bishops, "He who listens to you listens to me, and he who rejects you rejects me" (Luke 10:16). Jesus promised to guide his Church into all truth (John 16:12–13). We can have confidence that his Church teaches the truth of Christ.

THE STRUCTURE OF THE CHURCH

Jesus chose the apostles to be the earthly leaders of the Church. He gave them his own authority to teach and to govern—not as dictators, but as loving pastors and fathers. That is why Catholics call their spiritual leaders "father." In doing so we follow Paul's example: "I became your father in Jesus Christ through the gospel" (1 Cor. 4:15).

The apostles, fulfilling Jesus' will, ordained bishops, priests, and deacons and thus handed on their apostolic ministry to them—the fullest degree of ordination to the bishops, lesser degrees to the priests and deacons.

The Pope and Bishops
(CCC 880–883)

Jesus gave Peter special authority among the apostles (John 21:15–17) and signified this by changing his name from Simon to Peter, which means "rock" (John 1:42). He said Peter was to be the rock on which he would build his Church (Matt. 16:18).

In Aramaic, the language Jesus spoke, Simon's new name was *Kepha* (which means a massive rock). Later this name was translated into Greek as *Petros* (John 1:42) and into English as Peter. Christ gave Peter alone the "keys of the kingdom" (Matt. 16:19) and promised that Peter's decisions would be binding in heaven. He also gave similar power to the other apostles (Matt. 18:18), but only Peter was given the keys, symbols of his authority to rule the Church on earth in Jesus' absence.

Christ, the Good Shepherd, called Peter to be the chief shepherd of his Church (John 21:15–17). He gave Peter the task of strengthening the other apostles in their faith, ensuring that the faith of the Church would never go astray (Luke 22:31–32). Peter led the Church in proclaiming the gospel and making decisions (Acts 2:1– 41, 15:7–12).

Early Christian writings tell us that Peter's successors, the bishops of Rome (who from the earliest times have been called by the affectionate title of "pope," which means "papa"), continued to exercise Peter's ministry in the Church.

The pope is the successor to Peter as bishop of Rome. The world's other bishops are successors to the apostles in general.

HOW GOD SPEAKS TO US

As from the first, God speaks to his Church through the Bible and through sacred Tradition. To make sure we understand him, he guides the Church's teaching authority—the magisterium—so it always interprets the Bible and Tradition accurately. This is the gift of infallibility.

Like the three legs on a stool, the Bible, Tradition, and the magisterium are all necessary for the stability of the Church and to guarantee sound doctrine.

Sacred Tradition
(CCC 75–83)

Sacred Tradition should not be confused with mere traditions of men, which are more commonly called customs or disciplines. Jesus sometimes condemned customs or disciplines, but only if they were contrary to God's commands (Mark 7:8). He never condemned sacred Tradition, and he didn't even condemn all human tradition.

Sacred Tradition and the Bible are not different or competing revelations. They are two ways that the Church hands on the gospel. Apostolic teachings such as the Trinity, infant baptism, the inerrancy of the Bible, purgatory, and Mary's perpetual virginity have been most clearly taught through Tradition, although they are also implicitly present in (and not contrary to) the Bible. The Bible itself tells us to hold fast to Tradition, whether it comes to us in written or oral form (2 Thess. 2:15, 1 Cor. 11:2).

Sacred Tradition should not be confused with customs and disciplines, such as the rosary, priestly celibacy, and not eating meat on Fridays in Lent. These are good and helpful things, but they are not doctrines. Sacred Tradition preserves doctrines first taught by Jesus to the apostles and later passed down to us through the Church, under the leadership of the apostles' successors, the popes and the bishops.

Scripture
(CCC 101–141)

Scripture, by which we mean the Old and New Testaments, was inspired by God (2 Tim. 3:16). The Holy Spirit guided the biblical authors to write what he wanted them to write. "The inspired books teach the truth. 'Since therefore all that the inspired authors or sacred writers affirm should be regarded as affirmed by the Holy Spirit, we must acknowledge that the books of Scripture firmly, faithfully, and without error teach that truth which God, for the sake of our salvation, wished to see confided to the Sacred Scriptures'" (CCC 107, citing *Dei Verbum* 11).

Some Christians claim, "The Bible is all I need," but this notion is not taught in the Bible itself. In fact, the Bible teaches the contrary idea (2 Pet. 1:20–21, 3:15–16). The "Bible alone" theory was not believed by anyone in the early Church.

It is new, having arisen only in the 1500s during the Protestant Reformation. The theory is a "tradition of men" that nullifies the Word of God, distorts the true role of the Bible, and undermines the authority of the Church Jesus established (Mark 7:1–8).

Although popular with many "Bible Christian" churches, the "Bible alone" theory simply does not work in practice. Historical experience disproves it. Each year we see additional splintering among "Bible-believing" religions.

Today there are tens of thousands of competing denominations, each insisting its interpretation of the Bible is the correct one. The resulting divisions have caused untold confusion among millions of sincere but misled Christians. Just open up the Yellow Pages of your telephone book and see how many different denominations are listed, each claiming to go by the "Bible alone," but no two of them agreeing on exactly what the Bible *means*. We know this for sure: The Holy Spirit cannot be the author of this confusion (1 Cor. 14:33). God cannot lead people to contradictory beliefs because his truth is one. The conclusion? The "Bible alone" theory must be false.

The Magisterium
(CCC 85–87, 888–892)

Together the pope and the bishops form the teaching authority of the Church, which is called the magisterium (from the Latin for "teacher"). The magisterium, guided and protected from error by the Holy Spirit, gives us certainty in matters of doctrine. The Church is the custodian of the Bible and faithfully and accurately proclaims its message, a task which God has empowered it to do.

Keep in mind that the Church came before the New Testament, not the New Testament before the Church. Divinely-inspired members of the Church wrote the books of the New Testament, just as divinely-inspired writers had written the Old Testament, and the Church is guided by the Holy Spirit to guard and interpret the entire Bible, both Old and New Testaments.

Such an official interpreter is absolutely necessary if we are to understand the Bible properly. (We all know what the Constitution *says,* but we still need a Supreme Court to interpret what it *means*.) The magisterium is infallible when it teaches officially because Jesus promised to send the Holy Spirit to guide the apostles and their successors "into all truth" (John 16:12–13).

HOW GOD DISTRIBUTES HIS GIFTS

Jesus promised he would not leave us orphans (John 14:18) but would send the Holy Spirit to guide and protect us (John 15:26). He gave the sacraments to heal, feed, and strengthen us.

The seven sacraments —baptism, the Eucharist, penance (also called reconciliation or confession), confirmation, holy orders, matrimony, and the anointing of the sick—are not just symbols. They are signs that actually convey God's grace and love.

The sacraments were foreshadowed in the Old Testament by things that did not actually convey grace but merely symbolized it (circumcision, for example, prefigured baptism, and the Passover meal prefigured the Eucharist. When Christ came, he did not do away with symbols of God's grace. He super-naturalized them, energizing them with grace. He made them more than symbols.

God constantly uses material things to show his love and power. After all, matter is not evil. When he created the physical universe, everything God created was "very good" (Gen. 1:31). He takes such delight in matter that he even dignified it through his own Incarnation (John 1:14).

During his earthly ministry Jesus healed, fed, and strengthened people through humble elements such as mud, water, bread, oil, and wine. He could have performed his miracles directly, but he preferred to use material things to bestow his grace.

In his first public miracle Jesus turned water into wine, at the request of his mother, Mary (John 2:1–11). He healed a blind man by rubbing mud on his eyes (John 9:1–7). He multiplied a few loaves and fish into a meal for thousands (John 6:5–13). He changed bread and wine into his own body and blood (Matt. 26:26– 28). Through the sacraments he continues to heal, feed, and strengthen us.

Baptism
(CCC 1213–1284)

Because of original sin, we are born without grace in our souls, so there is no way for us to have fellowship with God. Jesus became man to bring us into union with his Father. He said no one can enter the kingdom of God unless he is first born of "water and the Spirit" (John 3:5)—this refers to baptism.

Through baptism we are born again, but this time on a spiritual level instead of a physical level. We are washed in the bath of rebirth (Titus 3:5). We are baptized into Christ's death and therefore share in his Resurrection (Rom. 6:3–7).

Baptism cleanses us of sins and brings the Holy Spirit and his grace into our souls (Acts 2:38, 22:16). And the apostle Peter is perhaps the most blunt of all: "Baptism now saves you" (1 Pet. 3:21). Baptism is the gateway into the Church.

Penance
(CCC 1422–1498)

Sometimes on our journey toward the heavenly promised land we stumble and fall into sin. God is always ready to lift us up and to restore us to grace-filled fellowship with him. He does this through the sacrament of penance (which is also known as confession or reconciliation, each term emphasizing a different element of the sacrament).

Jesus gave his apostles power and authority to reconcile us to the Father. They received Jesus' own power to forgive sins when he breathed on them and said, "Receive the Holy Spirit. Whose sins you forgive are forgiven them, and whose sins you retain are retained" (John 20:22–23).

Paul notes that "all this is from God, who has reconciled us to himself through Christ and given us the ministry of reconciliation. . . . We are ambassadors for Christ, as if God were appealing through us" (2 Cor. 5:18–20). Through confession to a priest, God's minister, we have our sins forgiven, and we receive grace to help us resist future temptations.

The Eucharist
(CCC 1322–1419)

Once we become members of Christ's family, he does not let us go hungry, but feeds us with his own body and blood through the Eucharist.

In the Old Testament, as they prepared for their journey in the wilderness, God commanded his people to sacrifice a lamb and sprinkle its blood on their doorposts, so the Angel of Death would pass by their homes. Then they ate the lamb to seal their covenant with God.

This lamb prefigured Jesus. He is the real "Lamb of God," who takes away the sins of the world (John 1:29). Through Jesus we enter into a New Covenant with God (Luke 22:20), who protects us from eternal death. God's Old Testament people ate the Passover lamb.

Now we must eat the Lamb that is the Eucharist. Jesus said, "Unless you eat my flesh and drink my blood you have no life within you" (John 6:53).

At the Last Supper he took bread and wine and said, "Take and eat. This is my body . . . This is my blood which will be shed for you" (Mark 14:22–24). In this way Jesus instituted the sacrament of the

Eucharist, the sacrificial meal Catholics consume at each Mass.

The Catholic Church teaches that the sacrifice of Christ on the cross occurred "once for all" it cannot be repeated (Heb. 9:28). Christ does not "die again" during Mass, but the very same sacrifice that occurred on Calvary is made present on the altar. That's why the Mass is not "another" sacrifice, but a participation in the same, once-for-all sacrifice of Christ on the cross.

Paul reminds us that the bread and the wine really become, by a miracle of God's grace, the actual body and blood of Jesus: "Anyone who eats and drinks without recognizing the body of the Lord eats and drinks judgment on himself" (1 Cor. 11:27–29).

After the consecration of the bread and wine, no bread or wine remains on the altar. Only Jesus himself, under the appearance of bread and wine, remains.

Confirmation
(CCC 1285–1321)

God strengthens our souls in another way, through the sacrament of confirmation. Even though Jesus' disciples received grace before his Resurrection, on Pentecost the Holy Spirit came to strengthen them with new graces for the difficult work ahead. Then they went out and preached the gospel fearlessly and carried out the mission Christ had given them. Later, they laid hands on others to strengthen them as well (Acts 8:14–17). Through confirmation you too are strengthened to meet the spiritual challenges in your life.

Matrimony
(CCC 1601–1666)

Most people are called to the married life rather than to the religious life or to life as a single person. Through the sacrament of matrimony God gives special graces to help married couples with life's difficulties, especially to help them raise their children as loving followers of Christ.

Marriage always involves three parties: the bride, the groom, and God. When two Christians receive the sacrament of matrimony, God is with them, witnessing and blessing their marriage covenant. For Catholics, God does this through the priest or deacon who presides at the wedding as the Church's witness.

A consumated sacramental marriage is permanent; only death can break it (Mark 10:1–12, Rom. 7:2–3, 1 Cor. 7:10–11). This holy union is a living symbol of the unbreakable relationship between Christ and his Church (Eph. 5:21–33).

Holy Orders
(CCC 1536–1600)

Others are called to share specially in Christ's priesthood. In the Old Covenant, even though Israel was a kingdom of priests (Exod. 19:6), the Lord called certain men to a special priestly ministry (Exod. 19: 22). In the New Covenant, even though Christians are a kingdom of priests (1 Pet. 2:9), Jesus calls certain men to a special priestly ministry (Rom. 15:15–16).

This sacrament is called holy orders. Through it priests are ordained and thus empowered to serve the Church (2 Tim. 1:6–7) as pastors, teachers, and spiritual fathers who heal, feed, and strengthen God's people—most importantly through preaching and the administration of the sacraments.

Anointing of the Sick
(CCC 1499–1532)

Priests care for us when we are physically ill. They do this through the sacrament known as the anointing of the sick. The Bible instructs us, "Is anyone among you suffering? He should pray. . . . Is any one among you sick? He should summon the presbyters [priests] of the Church, and they should pray over him and anoint him with oil in the name of the Lord, and the prayer of faith will save the sick person, and the Lord will raise him up. If he has committed any sins, he will be forgiven" (Jas. 5:14–15).

Anointing of the sick not only helps us endure illness, but it cleanses our souls and helps us prepare to meet God.

TALKING WITH GOD AND HIS SAINTS

One of the most important activities for a Catholic is prayer. Without it there can be no true spiritual life. Through personal prayer and the communal prayer of the Church, especially the Mass, we worship and praise God, we express sorrow for our sins, and we intercede on behalf of others (1 Tim. 2:1–4). Through prayer we grow in our relationship with Christ and with members of God's family (CCC 2663–2696).

This family includes all members of the Church, whether on earth, in heaven, or in purgatory. Since Jesus has only one body, and since death has no power to separate us from Christ (Rom. 8:38), Christians who are in heaven or who, before entering heaven, are being purified in purgatory by God's love (1 Cor. 3:12–15) are still part of the Body of Christ (CCC 962).

Jesus said the second greatest commandment is to "love your neighbor as yourself" (Matt. 22:39). Those in heaven love us more intensely than they ever could have loved us while on earth. They pray for us constantly (Rev. 5:8), and their prayers are powerful (Jas. 5:16, CCC 956, 2683, 2692). Our prayers to the saints in heaven, asking for their prayers for us, and their intercession with the Father do not undermine Christ's role as sole Mediator (1 Tim. 2:5). In asking saints in heaven to pray for us we follow Paul's instructions: "I urge that supplications, prayers, intercessions, and thanksgivings be made for everyone," for "this is good and pleasing to God our Savior" (1 Tim. 2:1–4).

All members of the Body of Christ are called to help one another through prayer (CCC 2647). Mary's prayers are especially effective on our behalf because of her relationship with her Son (John 2:1–11).

God gave Mary a special role (CCC 490–511, 963– 975). He saved her from all sin (Luke 1:28, 47), made her uniquely blessed among all women (Luke 1:42), and made her a model for all Christians (Luke 1:48). At the end of her life he took her, body and soul, into heaven—an image of our own resurrection at the end of the world (Rev. 12:1–2).

WHAT IS THE PURPOSE OF LIFE?

Old catechisms asked, "Why did God make you?" The answer: "God made me to know him, to love him, and to serve him in this world and to be happy with him forever in the next." Here, in just 26 words, is the whole reason for our existence. Jesus answered the question even more briefly: "I came so that [you] might have life and have it more abundantly" (John 10:10).

God's plan for you is simple. Your loving Father wants to give you all good things—especially eternal life. Jesus died on the cross to save us all from sin and the eternal separation from God that sin causes (CCC 599–623). When he saves us, he makes us part of his Body, which is the Church (1 Cor. 12:27–30). We thus become united with him and with Christians everywhere (on earth, in heaven, in purgatory).

What You Must Do to Be Saved

Best of all, the promise of eternal life is a gift, freely offered to us by God (CCC 1727). Our initial forgiveness and justification are not things we "earn" (CCC 2010). Jesus is the mediator who bridged the gap of sin that separates us from God (1 Tim. 2:5); he bridged it by dying for us. He has chosen to make us partners in the plan of salvation (1 Cor. 3:9).

The Catholic Church teaches what the apostles taught and what the Bible teaches: We are saved by grace alone, but not by faith alone (which is what "Bible Christians" teach; see Jas. 2:24).

When we come to God and are justified (that is, enter a right relationship with God), nothing preceding justification, whether faith or good works, *earns* grace. But then God plants his love in our hearts, and we should live out our faith by doing acts of love (Gal. 6:2).

Even though only God's grace enables us to love others, these acts of love please him, and he promises to reward them with eternal life (Rom. 2:6–7, Gal. 6:6–10). Thus good works are meritorious. When we first come to God in faith, we have nothing in our hands to offer him. Then he gives us grace to obey his commandments in love, and he rewards us with salvation when we offer these acts of love back to him (Rom. 2:6–11, Gal. 6:6–10, Matt. 25:34–40).

Jesus said it is not enough to have faith in him; we also must obey his commandments. "Why do you call me 'Lord, Lord,' but do not do the things I command?" (Luke 6:46, Matt. 7:21–23, 19:16–21).

We do not "earn" our salvation through good works (Eph. 2:8–9, Rom. 9:16), but our faith in Christ puts us in a special grace-filled relationship with God so that our obedience and love, combined with our faith, will be rewarded with eternal life (Rom. 2:7, Gal. 6:8–9).

Paul said, "God is the one who, for his good purpose, works in you both to desire and to work" (Phil. 2:13). John explained that "the way we may be sure that we know him is to keep his commandments. Whoever says, 'I know him,' but does not keep his

commandments is a liar, and the truth is not in him"
(1 John 2:3–4, 3:19–24, 5:3–4). Since no gift can be
forced on the recipient—gifts always can be reject-
ed—even after we become justified, we can throw
away the gift of salvation. We throw it away through
grave (mortal) sin (John 15:5–6, Rom. 11:22–23, 1
Cor. 15:1–2; CCC 1854–1863). Paul tells us, "The
wages of sin is death" (Rom. 6:23).

Read his letters and see how often Paul warned
Christians against sin! He would not have felt com-
pelled to do so if their sins could not exclude them
from heaven (see, for example, 1 Cor. 6:9–10, Gal.
5:19–21). Paul reminded the Christians in Rome that
God "will repay everyone according to his works:
eternal life for those who seek glory, honor, and
immortality through perseverance in good works, but
wrath and fury to those who selfishly disobey the
truth and obey wickedness" (Rom. 2:6–8).

Sins are nothing but evil works (CCC
1849–1850). We can avoid sins by habitually per-
forming good works. Every saint has known that the
best way to keep free from sins is to embrace regular
prayer, the sacraments (the Eucharist first of all), and
charitable acts.

Are You Guaranteed Heaven?

Some people promote an especially attractive idea:
All true Christians, regardless of how they live, have

an absolute assurance of salvation, once they accept Jesus into their hearts as "their personal Lord and Savior." The problem is that this belief is contrary to the Bible and constant Christian teaching.

Keep in mind what Paul told the Christians of his day: "If we have died with him [in baptism; see Rom. 6:3–4] we shall also live with him; if we persevere we shall also reign with him" (2 Tim. 2:11–12). If we do *not* persevere, we shall *not* reign with him. In other words, Christians can forfeit heaven (CCC 1861).

The Bible makes it clear that Christians have a moral assurance of salvation (God will be true to his word and will grant salvation to those who have faith in Christ and are obedient to him [1 John 3:19–24]), but the Bible does not teach that Christians have a guarantee of heaven. There can be no absolute assurance of salvation.

Writing to Christians, Paul said, "See, then, the kindness and severity of God: severity toward those who fell, but God's kindness to you, provided you remain in his kindness, otherwise you too will be cut off" (Rom. 11:22–23; Matt. 18:21–35, 1 Cor. 15:1–2, 2 Pet. 2:20–21).

Note that Paul includes an important condition: "provided you remain in his kindness." He is saying that Christians can lose their salvation by throwing it away. He warns, "Whoever thinks he is standing secure should take care not to fall" (1 Cor. 10:11–12).

If you are Catholic and someone asks you if you have been "saved," you should say, "I am redeemed by the blood of Christ, I trust in him alone for my salvation, and, as the Bible teaches, I am 'working out my salvation in fear and trembling' (Phil. 2:12), knowing that it is God's gift of grace that is working in me."

THE WAVE OF THE FUTURE

All the alternatives to Catholicism are showing themselves to be inadequate: the worn-out secularism that is everywhere around us and that no one any longer finds satisfying, the odd cults and movements that offer temporary community but no permanent home, even the other, incomplete brands of Christianity.

As our tired world becomes ever more desperate, people are turning to the one alternative they never really had considered: the Catholic Church. They are coming upon truth in the last place they expected to find it.

Never Popular, Always Attractive

How can this be? Why are so many people seriously looking at the Catholic Church for the first time? Something is pulling them toward it. That something is truth. This much we know: They are not

26

considering the claims of the Church out of a desire to win public favor. Catholicism, at least nowadays, is never popular. You cannot win a popularity contest by being a faithful Catholic. Our fallen world rewards the clever, not the good. If a Catholic is praised, it is for the worldly skills he demonstrates, not for his Christian virtues.

Although people try to avoid the hard doctrinal and moral truths the Catholic Church offers them (because hard truths demand that lives be changed), they nevertheless are attracted to the Church. When they listen to the pope and the bishops in union with him, they hear words with the ring of truth—even if they find that truth hard to live by.

When they contemplate the history of the Catholic Church and the lives of its saints, they realize there must be something special, maybe something supernatural, about an institution that can produce holy people such as St. Augustine, St. Thomas Aquinas, and Mother Teresa.

When they step off a busy street and into the aisles of an apparently empty Catholic church, they sense not a complete emptiness, but a presence. They sense that *Someone* resides inside, waiting to comfort them. They realize that the persistent opposition that confronts the Catholic Church—whether from nonbelievers or "Bible Christians" or even from people who insist on calling themselves Catholics—is a sign of the Church's divine origin (John 15:18–21).

And they come to suspect that the Catholic Church, of all things, is the wave of the future.

Incomplete Christianity Is Not Enough

Over the last few decades many Catholics have left the Church, many dropping out of religion entirely, many joining other churches. But the traffic has not been in only one direction.

The traffic toward Rome has increased rapidly. Today we are seeing more than a hundred and fifty thousand converts enter the Catholic Church each year in the United States, and in some other places, like the continent of Africa, there are more than a million converts to the Catholic faith each year. People of no religion, lapsed or inactive Catholics, and members of other Christian churches are "coming home to Rome." They are attracted to the Church for a variety of reasons, but the chief reason they convert is the chief reason *you* should be Catholic: The solid truth of the Catholic faith.

Our separated brethren hold much Christian truth, but not all of it. We might compare their religion to a stained glass window in which some of the original panes were lost and have been replaced by opaque glass: Something that was present at the beginning is now gone, and something that does not fit has been inserted to fill up the empty space. The unity of the original window has been marred. When, centuries ago, they split away from the Catholic Church, the theological ancestors of these Christians eliminated some authentic beliefs and added new ones of their own making. The forms of Christianity they established are really incomplete Christianity.

Only the Catholic Church was founded by Jesus, and only it has been able to preserve all Christian truth without any error—and great numbers of people are coming to see this.

YOUR TASKS AS A CATHOLIC

Your tasks as a Catholic, no matter what your age, are three:

Know your Catholic faith. You cannot live your faith if you do not know it, and you cannot share with others what you do not first make your own (CCC 429). Learning your Catholic faith takes some effort, but it is effort well spent because the study is, quite literally, infinitely rewarding.

Live your Catholic faith. Your Catholic faith is a public thing. It is not meant to be left behind when you leave home (CCC 2472). But be forewarned: Being a public Catholic involves risk and loss. You will find some doors closed to you. You will lose some friends. You will be considered an outsider. But, as a consolation, remember our Lord's words to the persecuted: "Rejoice and be glad, for your reward is great in heaven" (Matt. 5:12).

Spread your Catholic faith. Jesus Christ wants us to bring the whole world into captivity to the truth, and the truth is Jesus himself, who is "the way, and the truth, and the life" (John 14:6). Spreading the faith is a task not only for bishops, priests, and religious—it is a task for all Catholics (CCC 905).

Just before his Ascension, our Lord told his apostles, "Go, therefore, and make disciples of all nations, baptizing them in the name of the Father, and of the Son, and of the Holy Spirit, teaching them to observe all that I have commanded you" (Matt. 28:19–20).

If we want to observe all that Jesus commanded, if we want to believe all he taught, we must follow him through his Church. This is our great challenge—and our great privilege.

SUGGESTED READING

Catechism of the Catholic Church (Vatican City: Libreria Editrice Vaticana, 1994)

Henry G. Graham, *Where We Got the Bible* (San Diego: Catholic Answers, 1996)

William A. Jurgens, ed., *The Faith of the Early Fathers* (Collegeville: Liturgical Press, 1970)

Karl Keating, *Catholicism and Fundamentalism* (San Francisco: Ignatius Press, 1988)

Karl Keating, *What Catholics Really Believe: Setting the Record Straight* (San Francisco: Ignatius Press, 1995 [1992])

Father Mateo, *Refuting the Attack on Mary: A Defense of Marian Doctrines* (San Diego: Catholic Answers, 1993)

Ludwig Ott, *Fundamentals of Catholic Dogma* (Rockford: TAN Books and Publishers, 1974 [1960])

Frank Sheed and Maisie Ward, *Catholic Evidence Training Outlines* (Ann Arbor: Catholic Evidence Guild, 1992 [1948])

These books are available through Catholic Answers.

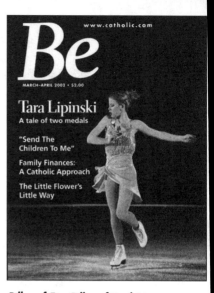